Pack a Picnic!

Written by Charlene Norman

CELEBRATION PRESS
Pearson Learning Group

Picnics are a fun way to share a meal with friends. Most picnics are meals you pack to take outdoors. When you pack a picnic, you should make good food choices. Good food choices help you feel, act, and grow in healthy ways.

These foods contain protein.

Your body needs protein to help you grow.
Protein helps heal injuries, too.

Foods such as chicken, beef, fish, eggs, cheese,
and soybeans contain protein.

3

These foods contain carbohydrates.

Carbohydrates give your body energy. Your body gets carbohydrates from some fruits and vegetables. These foods also contain lots of vitamins and minerals.

These foods contain fat.

at gives your body energy, too. A bit of fat
eeps eyes, skin, teeth, blood, and muscles
ealthy, but too much fat can be unhealthy.

5

Nutrition Facts

Serving Size 2 slices (56g)
Servings Per Container 10

Calories 140

Calories From Fat 10

Amount/serving	% Da
Total Fat 1.5g	
Saturated Fat 0g	
Cholesterol 0mg	
Sodium 280mg	

Vitamin A 0%	•	Vitamin C 0
Thiamin 15%	•	Riboflavin 8

*Percent Daily Values are based on a 2,000

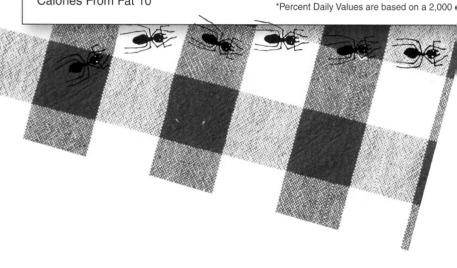

How much is too much? Read the nutrition labe
on foods to find out. Most food packages have
nutrition labels. The label tells you the amount o
protein, carbohydrates, fat, vitamins, or mineral.
in that food.

The Daily Value is the amount an adult should eat in one day. The percent shows how much of the Daily Value is in that food. Children should usually eat less than the Daily Value.

serving	% Daily Value*
Carbohydrate 26g	**9%**
ry Fiber 2g	**8%**
rs 1g	
n 4g	

6%   •   Iron 6%

%

Nutrition Facts
Serving Size 1/2 cup (114g)
Servings Per Container 4

Amount Per Serving

Calories 90   Calories From Fat 30

	% Daily Value*
Total Fat 3g	
Saturated Fat 0g	**5%**
Cholesterol 0mg	**0%**
Sodium 300mg	**0%**
Total Carbohydrate 13g	**13%**
Dietary Fiber 3g	**4%**
Sugars 3g	**12%**
Protein 3g	

Vitamin A 80%   •   Vitamin C 60%
Calcium 4%   •   Iron 4%

*Percent Daily Values are based on a 2,000 calorie diet.

What You Should Eat
to Keep Your Whole Body Healthy

Eat these foods . . .	. . . to keep these parts of your body healthy.
yellow, orange, and dark green vegetables; fruits; eggs; fish	eyes
milk, yogurt, cheese, spinach, eggs, dark green vegetables, nuts, seeds	bones and teeth
fruits and vegetables, cereal, milk, yogurt, beans, fish	heart, muscles
milk, yogurt, peanut butter, fruits, vegetables, seeds	skin

It's good to eat many different foods to keep all parts of your body healthy.

Here are some foods you can make to take along on your next picnic.

...ble Dip

1. Mix $\frac{1}{2}$ cup yogurt with 2 teaspoons yellow mustard and $\frac{1}{4}$ cup fat-free mayonnaise.

2. Dip radishes, cucumbers, broccoli, carrots, and green beans.

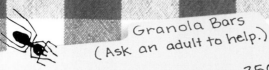

Granola Bars
(Ask an adult to help.)

1. Preheat an oven to 350°F.

2. Grease a 9-inch square pan.

3. Beat one egg.

4. In a bowl, mix the egg with 2 cups granola, $\frac{1}{4}$ cup firmly packed brown sugar, 1 teaspoon vanilla, and $\frac{1}{4}$ teaspoon cinnamon.

5. Press the mixture into the pan. Bake for 15 minutes.

6. Cool for 5 minutes.

7. Cut into bars.

Peanut Butter Worms

1. In a bowl, mix $\frac{1}{2}$ cup honey, $\frac{1}{2}$ cup creamy peanut butter, 1 cup nonfat dry milk, and 1 cup rolled oats.

2. Roll into worm shapes. Eat on carrot slices.

Your body needs liquids. So take plenty of water on your picnic. For a special treat, make a Purple Cow—half grape juice, half ginger ale with a scoop of nonfat vanilla ice milk.

On your next picnic, make good food choices.
Enjoy your power-packed picnic!